NINE SERIES

The Opposite of Grieving

Hugh McMillan
Neil Young
Jessamine O'Connor

Published by Nine Pens

2023

www.ninepens.co.uk

All rights reserved: no part of this book may be reproduced without the publisher's permission.

The rights of the authors Hugh McMillan, Jessamine O'Connor and Neil Young to be identified as the authors of this work has been asserted by them in accordance with the Copyright, Designs and Patents act 1988.

ISBN: 978-1-7391517-9-9

NS 007

Hugh McMillan
7   Hole in the Sky
8   Glass
9   Diverted to Split
10 Miracle
11 The Walks
12 Yellow Horses
14 The Girls in the Woods
16 Flying
17 Dream

Neil Young
21 Sappho Sends a Memo to the Laddies
23 Andromeda's Flight
24 Sparta Casuals Plot their Comeback Tour
25 Ares Writes a Letter to His Teenage Self
26 Ferrymen Ballot for Strike
28 Echo
29 Hecate on Dogs
30 Anarchy on Lesbos
31 Icarus Syndrome

Jessamine O'Connor
35 Sky Burial on a Peckham High-Rise
37 Cillíní
39 Blackcurrant Picking
41 For the Record
43 Passenger
46 Notes on John
47 Stress Test
50 My Flickering Bathroom
52 The Opposite of Grieving

Hugh McMillan

Hugh's latest collection 'Haphazardly in the Starless Night' was published in 2021. In 2021 he was editor of the SPL's anthology 'Best Scottish Poems'. He edits for Drunk Muse Press.

Hole in the Sky

A half empty train and
the north of England flicking
by in deep shades of green
and wild hawthorn.

I am sipping wine
and you are carefully judging
the smoothie you drink.
Food is a map we spread

out and navigate by:
we sometimes get lost there.
The sun is on your face, you
are smiling, but I have never

been more scared.
Can we make this day
a paradigm? One to fall
back on through the clouds.

Glass

The cold seeps
through the windows
of Whitby.
The sea is wild
and beautiful
today you say,

it is shattering
on the walls
and moles and jetties.
At night the strings
of bulbs are twisted
over and over

by the fingers
of the wind.
While you sleep
I walk
the long pier,
each bench bears

a story and
they jut into
the gleaming heart
of the ocean,
the young, the old,
the taken.

Later you shop
for jet but you
are glass
coming down
the steps, light
is through you.

Diverted to Split

Somewhere
in the unscarred
skies, in a fabulous
scaffold of blue

the way was parted,
some piece of muscle,
like thin fabric gave out
just like that, a wee,

very wee thing, like
life in fact. Imagine
lying streaked
with the sun on the shore,

draw me
a map of the Adriatic
from above,
in cloud white as bone.

Light is a dream
of breathlessness,
and only an inch
from sleep.

Miracle

The sun is here
blinkering
the unwary eye.
Even now at the turn

of winter it makes
flowers into plates
of gold, pebbles to glass.
I am writing a small

tribute to someone
I love, it is right
every moment
should have its ceremony,

every blaze and flicker.
It takes a million
years for energy
to reach from the centre

of the sun
to the surface,
then 8.6 seconds
to come to us.

Imagine that,
walking through
ancient light into the wreckage
of another year.

The Walks

Every day I walk round
the fields past the bench
and the hut, over the gate
and through the avenue of trees
that groan in the wind.

All this year my daughter
has walked with me,
in that hand-me-down parka
with its enveloping furry hood.
Mostly I watch her trainers

moving over the ground.
She doesn't stumble but glides
above, she is so light. Her face
is pointed to the canopy
of branches, to the sun

breaking in. I know her face,
it is beautiful, but I suppose
our minds are closed to one
another, no matter how much
we love or want. I tell myself

these days are a blessing.
Here we are again, at this junction
of thorn and sap. One day she'll keep
on. She surely must, she will take
a road, and I will turn on my step.

Yellow Horses

A friend leads me to
the Navajo legend of the horses,
how they were corralled
into the four corners of the world,
white horses to the east,
turquoise horses to the south,
yellow horses to the west,
and spotted horses to the north,
the colours of the compass,

the colours of morning, noon,
afternoon, and night.
She writes that her granddaughter
arrived on an abalone horse
in the early winter morning.
I'm standing here below
trees which stretch like fingers
at the end of a day in this bit
of Scotland and I start crying- oh yes

it is because of my own problems,
but let us not discount the miracle
of that birth across the ocean, and the horses too,
in my head like the horses my daughters
rode when they were young.
We are all touched by the same sky,
the same misery and joys,
the coming and goings; it all happens under
the same shell coloured sky

The Girls in the Wood

There's a mob of small girls
who roam the woods here.
You can hear distant calls
like birds or monkeys,
but it is rare to see them.

Folk who do are eager to pass
the knowledge on - almost
in hushed tones they say,
'yes we maybe spied them under
a bridge wading in green water',

or, 'I'm sure I caught a glimpse
by the old deer hide,
they were wearing red wellingtons'.
I think it is the mob of small girls
in the wood who built that shelter

made of intricately laced branches,
hazel twisted into ribs and logs
inside for tiny seats.
They are never there when I pass,
though often there is a slight

stir as if the place has just
emptied and I imagine
in the shadows between trees

those leaves wet with rain
are eyes gleaming.

Whatever it is about the mob
of small girls in the wood,
they are not faeries or ghosts,
though sometimes
when I hear cries lost in the wind

I let myself feel they are.
That is ridiculous: in the village
these girls are well known.
But in the woods!
When people talk of it,

the smeddum, the indivisibility,
it takes them back.
Even the hardest of them,
who have lost the most,
it takes them back.

Flying

All these heads above orange seats
like fruit in a crate.
Lydia says what's the difference

between a mucky bus stop
and a lobster after breast surgery?
She is 21 and studying philosophy.

Through the pill of the window
clouds bubble, form palms and knuckles.
It is April 2023. In my book someone

has just been eaten by a shark.
There is plenty of wine left
but everyone is longing for that swamp,

the ground. The ground is overrated-
my manifesto. I say let's keep juddering
thermals between sleep and unfounded

optimism. Here where my daughters
frame a porthole of pure
blue horizon, riding our luck.

Dream

A wide expanse of grass,
a stream meandering between
tiny trees. It is Versailles
below a pearl white sky.
I know this because we are
dressed in paper ribbons
of the most flamboyant kind,
yellow, red, aquamarine.
We waft in a breeze laced
with hyacinth and jasmine.
How posh we must be
to pirouette here half asleep
like Kings and Queens. Here
you are, so I know the gardens
are given over to poets between
three and four in the morning.
Good day! Good night!
See how the brain gathers us all
and shakes us out
on random chessboard lawns.

Neil Young

Neil hails from west Belfast and now lives in north-east Scotland. He worked as a labourer, kitchen-porter and stage-hand before becoming a journalist. His latest collections include Shrapnel (Poetry Salzburg, 2019) and After the Riot (Nine Pens Press, 2021). Neil is co-founder of The Poets' Republic magazine and Drunk Muse Press.

Sappho Sends a Memo to the Laddies

Don't go summoning me, sad poets.
I'm on a long lunch, fair sick of your stuff,

you mystic flakes and academics,
I've read more meaningful buttock fluff;

I won't be signing off or finessing
your epics. Try Erato, I hear

she's cheap. She's fast. For half a credit
she'd slop in any Oxbridger's ear:

Classical posers, I'd get a bad rep
if word got about I'd sponsored your verse

and end up looking like Caliope.
Botoxed. Face like a Trojan hearse.

Call this poetry, it's Gravesian guff,
posh boys' clubbiness, coded speak

for lit-fest lads and Times reviewers
to spout their Latin, strut their Greek.

Your convolutions are useless to those
who use up arms and brains then croke

too young or fluke it into old age.
(You might have heard about those folk)

and leave all that Muse-bothering fancy
to dreeps who write for prizes and fame.

On that wee note, are you still here?
Come back when you've grown bollocks again.

Andromeda's Flight

By now Andromeda was well pissed off:
Chained to a rock by the king, her DAD,
as sacrifice to a big sea beast
with a taste for local peasantry - bad enough!
Betrayed by fiance Phineas in her hour of need?
Feartie Phineas, what a fanny!
None of it what you'd call 'progressive stuff'.

Ye gods be thanked for Perseus,
have-a-go hero, epic looks,
smashing her shackles and didn't quit
until he'd salamied the serpent.
Here's the rub:
It's not as if she wasn't grateful, OMG,
but what's this claiming her as bride
from her repentant ("go fuck yerself") dad
and weaponising that Medusa's head
he balled around in his man-bag
so he could fossilise her ex?
Marriage to him could be a drag.

It had to be said: "Perseus, lad,
you're fit as fuck with your golden hair
but there are plenty more
damsels chained to crags in the sea
and one for you - it's just not me.
Lend me those winged sandals you wear,
I'm told Troy rocks this time of year."

Sparta Casuals Plot their Comeback Tour

Soon as we've drank this Helot's blood,
scoffed those magic manitária
Leonidas' nephew fetched
back from his gap year
we're trashing Thebes high street,
including shops,
whether the Wags
give us permission or not.
Then we'll do Corinth;
remember to pack
an armpit flannel
and clean loin cloth,
we'll all be sharing
an overnight cart,
it could get stinky and stuff.

Massalia, Chalcis,
this is payback
for calling Tyrtaeus a wuss
just cos he writes poems.
Athenians, get your
Snowflake-lads tooled up.

Chaps, remember our chants:
'Two Med wars and one Aegean Cup',
'We're Sparta till we die'.

Give 'em Hades
right after you've waxed your chests.

Ares Writes a Letter to His Teenage Self

Step away from that full-length mirror, kid,
untie those weights,
they won't make it grow any longer,
you'll end up lurching through manhood.

I know your parents have slated you
for god of war and bloodshed
but you might want to think about
what comes when
you need another skill-set.

Try reading a scroll that hasn't been scratched
by old men hero-worshipping youth,
avoid other lads like yourself,
stop leper-baiting - it's not their fault.

Consider this: Achilles would follow
a one-legged boar with septic teeth
for the sake of a headline or two
but is that the kind of flattery you want?
He's going to meet a bad end.

Ares, feller, there's more to youth
than spearing dogs for target practice
and telling your mates you're not gay.
Eat some berries,
all that red meat
could give you eternal bad breath.

Ferrymen Ballot for Strike

What you need to know is there'd be no myths
without us, the key workers

who've kept the Underworld flowing
through plagues and carnage for aeons.

Folk would be tripping over the dead in the street
without us lasses and lads of the Styxworkers Union,

Olympus would be a hillock. It only looks good
because we keep the lights out in the abyss.

Are we fabled? No. Glory-hunters? No.
Are we the sort for extravagant gestures,

lashing ourselves to masts
or slaying phantasmagorical beasts?

We're the scene-shifters, legion of prompters,
eternal nail-thumpers who keep A-listers A.

Achilles would be a provincial thug minus
our toil, Paris living at home with his mum.

All this and ne'er a Drachma's rise
since Agamemnon was in short togas.

If Pluto would have it we're not averse
to Olympian arbitration. But we're deadlocked.

Remind that flake-head Orpheus this is a picket line:
cross us – even for love – and he's a scab.

Echo

There she drifts, poor Echo,
typecast forever
as a moon-eyed lass who chased
an anaemic fop and lost.

There's the villain, Narcissus,
not quite the lad that mums
warn daughters about,
hardly sex 'n' drugs n rock 'n' roll,
his face is caked in products,
hair's by L'Oreal.

The fable-makers got it wrong.
The way that craggy ancients do.
Undress themselves
when they write of others.
Narcissus is a byword for tosser,
Echo became an encore.

Hecate on Dogs

Our superior wisdom
has nothing on dogs,
we've overthought ourselves
into a cul-de-sac.

Be more like dogs.
We might not choose
their doggy foibles -
dig holes for no
discernible purpose,
eat sticks,
rejoice at defecating on lawns,
shag passing
strangers in the park
then just 'move on'
with a shake of the tail,
howl at the sky
or somersault at letterboxes
for sport
at the postie's step

but think of it:
when did you see
a dog headbutt the wall?
Dogs don't do psycho-drama.
Dogs don't need to block tweets.

Anarchy on Lesbos

Sappho woke with a knackered lyre,
base all smashed where she'd tripped on it, pissed,
her hangover throbbed, her mood was dire,
she plucked the strings with an open fist
and WOW! what noise, what sound was this?

The other Muses weren't so impressed.
"You're out of control, give it a rest,"
they raged, but Sapph wouldn't be put off,
"Up yours," she volleyed, "I've had enough
of taking lessons from blue-rinse toffs
when all you play is ancient junk."

She slashed her robe, turned up her amp
and that's how Sappho invented punk.

Icarus Syndrome

Auden was right, both wrong and right
when he said of Breugel's Icarus
crashing from an over-blue sky that
'everything turns away
Quiet leisurely from the disaster; the ploughman may
Have heard the splash, the forsaken cry
But for him it was not an important failure'
Yes, their eyes are not so much averted
as disdainful of the sudden and small
and yes, it is survival drilled
by observance of the mundane
that sends humanity stumbling and dazed
each hour of the everyday.
But there was work to be done as well:
the ploughman's job to feed his young and harvest grain,
the ship perhaps with wool and wine,
and, hell, big hungry towns don't wait
for some vainglorious clown
who's strapped on wings to high-five the Sun,
who mocked the drudge of civic tasks for a shot at fame.
Icarus drops not from great height
but from delusions he's The One
much like loud stars of our own time
except we'd pause the scene, repeat,
the moment's never passed: he'd tweet
his freak celebrity now
till his face went splat
then tweet no more.

Jessamine O'Connor

Jessamine moved from Dublin to the Sligo Roscommon border in 1999. Her collection 'Silver Spoon' is published by Salmon Poetry. She is an editor with Drunk Muse Press, on the panel of The Poet's Republic, and runs Co:Mon, an annual Countdown festival.

Sky Burial on a Peckham High-Rise

The only flight we will ever take
together, the three of us
and the first thing you do on arrival
is leave,
you leave us for hours
with strangers
and when you land back
get straight at it, gouge out
on the couch and only come round eventually
to my fury -
this was meant to be a holiday, and besides
you didn't even keep me any

In a few days it's forgotten
when vaguely in my peripheral vision
suddenly the lump of your body
as it's dragged out to the landing.
They explain slowly, how you can't call an ambulance
here, because the police follow,
that they always leave the OD's outside
at someone else's door

Propped four floors up at a grey brick wall
in the lilac twilight with blueing lips, not breathing,
you look so peaceful
I start screaming.
There's a dark satisfaction in slapping

your flaccid face, like returning an unwanted gift.
Hitting harder, I hear myself beg
wake up wake up wake up
but you won't

Lights swing and swoop across the car-park
far below, wink blue and orange and I'm wrenched off you,
pulled inside, the door held shut, and hushed. We listen

You are left out, exposed
to the sky, crows and paramedics

Through the hours that follow
hearing nothing, you are both dead and alive.
Not knowing which, you can be either
at the same time. Our child sleeps -
simultaneously in a state of having a father,
and not

Cillíní

These cillíní
   are at chest-height

So we can open our arms
   widen our eyes

Inhale
   this moonlit grief

Feel
   the spade in our hands

See it slice
   through the earth

Lift the weight of that hole
   hold it

Bend down, kneel
   and place the child

Alone, into the opened
   ground

Breathe deep
   what that means

Listen –
   the cillíní are singing

Directly
   to your heart

a response to Tommy Weir's photography exhibition; Cillín. Unmarked burial grounds across Ireland where unbaptised babies and others were buried until recently, often by the fathers or male relatives during the night

Blackcurrant Picking

Crouched in bushes
plucking
blackcurrants in the heavy evening
one by one by one by –
    only the darkest
        this is methodical
and should be meditative
or something

Shiny clusters pick and pop
slowly crawl up the colander walls
accumulating
    tiny berry
      on tiny berry
but it's not quite like that

You're back in that exact old feeling
of immersion
      swirling
    surgical   alchemy
a sudden stench of disinfectant
nip   pause   gag   and taste
    in the base of your throat

Hurrying away the evidence
as focus twists to
maximum

    magnification
every detail erupting
a richness in all things
    depth
love for the shock of existence
parading through your circulatory system
all trumpets and sequins and arms high

    it's so quick
    the journey

and suddenly you're here in the bushes
rummaging for fruit
aware of your glaringly easy life
        all the lucky corners
with fingerprints stained purple and midgies
itching for blood, alone in the bushes this once

Allow yourself to stop
be nostalgic
for what you swear you don't want

For the Record
to David O'Hagan

When we fought like siblings
over the TV, over everything
and I ran telling on you –

When I pounded the walls
or floors of my bedrooms, screaming
turn it down
then came borrowing the same records
not long after, records I still have
on loan -

When I pinned that dating agency sign
on your bedroom door
to make it clear
my mother could do so much better -

When I embarked on my determined march
astray, and you waited up
to see me safe, but not to judge -

When then later you calmly took us in
treating the baby to late night dancing
and pushchair rides through the park
returning gleefully each day to announce
how the yummy mummies did not believe
you could be a grandad, and I scoffed

though you were just 44 –

When you came with me to court
then brought us on that river boat, bought scones
with jam and cream and we watched the water
until that's what I remember –

When you travel for hours
to proudly attend one of many boring events
or buy my books to send to people
like they must be good enough –

When thirty years later
you still wait up –

It should be known
that when I fought and argued
and moaned and challenged you
relentlessly over all those years
it was only because
I knew I could

Passenger

Paths slip past me, sitting sideways,
blue then grey then blue again.
The window like a cinema screen,
watching the rhythm of the rooftop light
switching quietly on, then off,
surprised by a blip of siren sometimes

but mostly silence, illuminating people passing
who nearly all turn to stare, still walking,
their faces flash with fleeting worry,
abruptly woken but go blank again just as quick.
Some stop, twitch, cross themselves
and search in the window

but I know I sit behind tinted glass
so can just look blank-faced back,
despising you for all the theatrics
strapped to the stretcher beside me
and me expected to go with you
for being the only other woman

when you'd horrified me
back then in the flat: suddenly there's roaring
and he's banged out the door
and we're all on our feet
un-used to dramatics.
I'm the last to cop-on to what's happened.

Palms up, you're standing, face changed, no boots,
your pretty feet striped in tights
on the dirty kitchen lino,
half a white mug on the counter,
handle-side jagged
and lacquered in what I slowly gather is blood.

Your left hand rolling with a red that floods to the floor
and The Lads are all action; phoning, deep breaths,
panicking, out of depth.
I feel frozen – what the fuck are you at? –
you stream off down the corridor
and are still flung on the bed when the ambulance men come.

Bending into your foil-papered room
in strangely tidy uniforms,
bigger than the door, they can't both get in.
We're all crowding, cajoling you from the hall,
they've got more calls, they say,
when you won't get up and go with them.

They back away, and I share their scorn, but they're leaving
you face down, leaking blood into the duvet
so we haul you up
and you let yourself be led outside
       and I let myself be put in with you
              and they close the doors tight after us.

We sway along the roads in the blue and grey,
your eyes are running black into your ears,
your perfect face is crunched and creased,
you always seemed to find everything so easy
and I'd come to hate your likeability,
but you did this to show him – what does that say?

In the hospital you're kept horizontal,
a doctor talks to you sternly, tiredly.
Sitting by your head, we must look close,
I'm distracting, making jokes, and you laugh
in pools, between remembering;
he wouldn't take you back.

I hold your clean hand, keep you from looking
when the doctor hunches over the other side
and pulls and pushes the needle roughly
through the loose flaps of your wrist.
I try not to, but watch each stitch, and think
who would have thought you'd do something like this?

Notes on John

Their Peckham squat declared
nobody here but us chickens -
he was vegan for years there and used to knit
for days on end, then unravel it all
and start again

and on the long walk behind the hearse
his friend I hadn't seen in 25 years said
when they got a council flat
he wouldn't get up in time for his key
and refused to pay for one to be cut

so every time he came back first
in the morning from a party
he'd have to kick down the door to get in
until eventually
there was no door left

Stress Test
for Sally in Sligo cardio

There's a rhythmic delicacy to these sketches
projecting from my circulatory system, fascinating
for a first-timer – it's hard to take my eyes off them
once the sparkling woman with the Scots bloom
in her vowels scratches patches of my torso
apologetically, with a swab or is it
a toothbrush - bristles
on ribcage
feel almost like stubble -
and I hoist my t-shirt high and laugh
about being glad to have worn the Good Bra
the one with the gold flecks and correct measurements
because I'd been warned: good bra, comfortable shoes
and these shoes are a perfect ugly match for the grey
gluey pads sticking skin to wires to machine
and with this all done she demonstrates
how to walk, where to rest my hands
not grip
what to expect
and when to stop

I walk slowly, watch the squiggles
travel leftwards, study numbers which mean nothing
to me, feet speeding - thighs catching - hips barely keeping up
lean into the tilt of the moving track and hope
when sweat begins to brew

that my pores don't fill
with last night's drink
emitting that stink into our air
but she doesn't mention anything like that
only points out the extra beats with splayed fingers
the way you'd point to an unusual butterfly
in the garden
    reassures me
these are nothing to worry about
  - did you feel that? No -
straps the Velcro round my bicep
blows it up and up, cold stethoscope
at the popping part
read, release
perfect

I slog up the treadmill hill
breathing damply through a plastic mask
nose just jutting over, chatting – trying to chat
– gasping
before admitting
that'll do
slowing down and stepping off. The floor swims
like a boat, she says, that's exactly how it is
so I sit and watch the jagged scribbles
continue bumpily, regular and irregular
delighted with myself
for owning this good blood pressure
even under such conditions as an insomniac hangover

and facemask, proud of my pumping heart and veins
in much the same way as being proud of ancestors
who you had no influence on
whatsoever

The map keeps writing itself without me
curling in raspberry ripple folds to the floor
black trails tracking where my pulse has just been
but looking a lot more like streams trickling
endlessly alongside each other
on and on and on
across rocky ground
learning during this test that
abnormal rhythm is fairly ordinary
not usually dangerous and really just the electrical system
being a wild expanse full of butterflies
beating their beautiful wings

My Flickering Bathroom

At 4.15
in the morning
the bathroom is
        having a fit
    with me inside it
             flashes of black
then   bright
        then   black
    irregular
        as a   heart beat
    chaotic
          as a life
            well lived

I sit and piss
        strobe lights
               pungent
     sweat
       vaporub
  smoke
       dancefloors
      tents
   vans   fields
cubicles
    holding wraps
         pills
     worse

```
              exploding       ribcage
                                        flash
                        wait
black
                  flash
            wait
black                     flash    bright
                  wait
                        wait
                                        wait

                              has it?
                  has it?
      maybe
              finally
the lightbulb
has settled
down
```

The Opposite of Grieving

is I'll lace up my boots
darken my eyes
wear a short skirt
and go out dancing

it won't be a rave
I don't have one to go to
but there's a punk gig
booked months ago

months before this
where I can reach my fists high
be crushed and lifted
and held by the moshpit

wishing him all good things
holding on to that brightness
bringing him with me
saying goodbye

www.ingramcontent.com/pod-product-compliance
Lightning Source LLC
Chambersburg PA
CBHW021133080526
44587CB00012B/1275